ODE TO APHRODITE

THE
POEMS & FRAGMENTS
OF SAPPHO

C000050599

Read & Co.

Copyright © 2021 Wine Dark Press

This edition is published by Wine Dark Press,
an imprint of Read & Co.

This book is copyright and may not be
reproduced or copied in any way without the
express permission of the publisher in writing.

British Library Cataloguing-in-Publication Data
A catalogue record for this book is available
from the British Library.

Read & Co. is part of Read Books Ltd.
For more information visit
www.readandcobooks.co.uk

'The mind of Sappho runs through
all literature like a spangled thread.'

—HENRY DE VERE STACPOOLE

"If all the poets and all the lovers of poetry should be asked to name the most precious of the priceless things which time has wrung in tribute from the triumphs of human genius, the answer which would rush to every tongue would be "The Lost Poems of Sappho."

—BLISS CARMEN

"Sappho, with that gloriole of ebon hair
on calmèd brows—O poet-woman! None
forgoes the leap, attaining the repose."

—E. B. Browning

"Sappho who broke off a fragment
of her soul for us to guess at."

—BLISS CARMEN

CONTENTS

FRAGMENTS

Translated by Henry De Vere Stacpoole

AN INTRODUCTION

―――――――

By H. De Vere Stacpoole

I

Sappho lies remote from us, beyond the fashions and the ages, beyond sight, almost beyond the wing of Thought, in the world's extremest youth.

To thrill the imagination with the vast measure of time between the world of Sappho and the world of the Great War, it is quite useless to express it in years, one must express it in æons, just as astronomers, dealing with sidereal distances, think, not in miles, but in light years.

Between us and Sappho lie the Roman Empire and the age of Christ, and beyond the cross the age of Athenian culture, culminating in the white flower of the Acropolis.

Had she travelled she might have visited
Nineveh before its destruction by Cyaxares,
or watched the Phœnicians set sail on their
African voyage at the command of Nechos. She
might have spoken with Draco and Jeremiah the
Prophet and the father of Gautama the founder
of Buddhism. For her the Historical Past, which
is the background of all thought, held little but
echoes, voices, and the forms of gods, and the
immediate present little but Lesbos and the
Ægean Sea, whose waters had been broken by the
first trireme only a hundred and fifty years before
her birth.

II

Men call her the greatest lyric poet that the
world has known, basing their judgment on the
few perfect fragments that remain of her song.
But her voice is more than the voice of a lyric
poet, it is the voice of a world that has been, of a
freshness and beauty that will never be again, and
to give that voice a last touch of charm remains

the fact that it comes to us as an echo.

For of Sappho's poetry not a single vestige remains that does not come to us reflected in the form of a quotation from the works of some admirer, some one captured by her beauty or her wisdom or the splendour of her verse, or some one, like Herodian or Apollonius the sophist of Alexandria, who takes it to exhibit the æolic use of words or accentuation, or Hephæstion, to give an example of her choriambic tetrameters.

Only one complete poem comes to us, the Hymn to Aphrodite quoted by Dionysius of Halicarnassus, and one almost complete, the Ode to Anactoria, quoted by Longinus; all other quotations are fragments: a few lines, a few words, a word, the merest traces.

What fate gave us the shipping lists of Homer, yet denied us Sappho; preserved the *Lexicon Græcum Iliadis et Odysseæ* of Apollonius, yet cut the song to Anactoria short, and reduced the song of the orchard to three lines? or decided that Sophists and Grammarians, exhibiting dry-as-dust truths, should be a medium between her and us?

Some say that her works were burned at Constantinople, or at Rome, by the Christians, and what we know of the early Christians lends colour to the statement. Some that they were burned by the Byzantine emperors and the poems of Gregory Nazianzen circulated in their place.

* * * * *

But whatever the fate it failed in its evil intention. Sappho remains, eternal as Sirius, and it is doubtful if her charm and her hold upon the world would have been strengthened by the full preservation of her work.

As it is, added to the longing which all great art inspires, we have the longing inspired by suggestion. That lovely figure belonging to the feet she shows us "crossed by a broidered strap of Lydian work," would it have been as beautiful unveiled as imagined? Did she long for maidenhood? Why did the swallow trouble her, and what did the daughter of Cyprus say to her in a dream?

There is not a fragment of Sappho that is not surrounded in the mind of the reader by the rainbow of suggestion. Just as the gods draped the human form to give desire imagination, so, perhaps, some god and no fate has all but hidden the mind of Sappho.

III

Looking at it in another way one might fancy that all the demons of malignity and destruction had conspired to destroy and traduce: to destroy the works and traduce the character of the poet.

The game of defamation was begun in Athens in the age of corruption by lepers, and carried on through the succeeding ages by their kind, till Welcker came with his torch and showed these gibbering ghosts standing on nothing and with nothing in their hands.

Colonel Mure tried to put Welcker's torch out, and only burned his fingers. Comparetti snuffed it, only to make it burn the brighter. But bright or dim, the torch was only intended to show the lepers. Sappho shines by her own light in the minutest fragments of her that remain—

Fragments whose deathless energy, like the energy of radium, has vivified literature in all ages and times.

SAPPHICS

By Algernon Charles Swinburne

All the night sleep came not upon my eyelids,
Shed not dew, nor shook nor unclosed a feather,
Yet with lips shut close and with eyes of iron
    Stood and beheld me.

Then to me so lying awake a vision
Came without sleep over the seas and touched me,
Softly touched mine eyelids and lips; and I too,
    Full of the vision,

Saw the white implacable Aphrodite,
Saw the hair unbound and the feet unsandalled
Shine as fire of sunset on western waters;
    Saw the reluctant

Feet, the straining plumes of the doves that drew her,
Looking always, looking with necks reverted,
Back to Lesbos, back to the hills whereunder
    Shone Mitylene;

Heard the flying feet of the Loves behind her
Make a sudden thunder upon the waters,
As the thunder flung from the strong unclosing
    Wings of a great wind.

So the goddess fled from her place, with awful
Sound of feet and thunder of wings around her;
While behind a clamour of singing women
    Severed the twilight.

Ah the singing, ah the delight, the passion!
All the Loves wept, listening; sick with anguish,
Stood the crowned nine Muses about Apollo;
    Fear was upon them,

While the tenth sang wonderful things they knew not.
Ah the tenth, the Lesbian! the nine were silent,
None endured the sound of her song for weeping;
    Laurel by laurel,

Faded all their crowns; but about her forehead,
Round her woven tresses and ashen temples
White as dead snow, paler than grass in summer,
    Ravaged with kisses,

Shone a light of fire as a crown for ever.
Yea, almost the implacable Aphrodite
Paused, and almost wept; such a song was that song.
    Yea, by her name too

Called her, saying, "Turn to me, O my Sappho;"
Yet she turned her face from the Loves, she saw not
Tears for laughter darken immortal eyelids,
    Heard not about her

Fearful fitful wings of the doves departing,
Saw not how the bosom of Aphrodite
Shook with weeping, saw not her shaken raiment,
    Saw not her hands wrung;

Saw the Lesbians kissing across their smitten
Lutes with lips more sweet than the sound of lute-strings,
Mouth to mouth and hand upon hand, her chosen,
    Fairer than all men;

Only saw the beautiful lips and fingers,
Full of songs and kisses and little whispers,
Full of music; only beheld among them
    Soar, as a bird soars

Newly fledged, her visible song, a marvel,
Made of perfect sound and exceeding passion,
Sweetly shapen, terrible, full of thunders,
    Clothed with the wind's wings.

Then rejoiced she, laughing with love, and scattered
Roses, awful roses of holy blossom;
Then the Loves thronged sadly with hidden faces
    Round Aphrodite,

Then the Muses, stricken at heart, were silent;
Yea, the gods waxed pale; such a song was that song.
All reluctant, all with a fresh repulsion,
    Fled from before her.

All withdrew long since, and the land was barren,
Full of fruitless women and music only.
Now perchance, when winds are assuaged at sunset,
    Lulled at the dewfall,

By the grey sea-side, unassuaged, unheard of,
Unbeloved, unseen in the ebb of twilight,
Ghosts of outcast women return lamenting,
    Purged not in Lethe,

Clothed about with flame and with tears, and singing
Songs that move the heart of the shaken heaven,
Songs that break the heart of the earth with pity,
    Hearing, to hear them.

ODE TO APHRODITE

POEMS

Translated by John Myres O'Hara

The following poems
where first published in
The Poems of Sappho, 1907

ODE TO
APHRODITE

―――――――

Aphrodite, subtle of soul and deathless,
Daughter of God, weaver of wiles, I pray thee
Neither with care, dread Mistress, nor with anguish,
    Slay thou my spirit!

But in pity hasten, come now if ever
From afar of old when my voice implored thee,
Thou hast deigned to listen, leaving the golden
    House of thy father

With thy chariot yoked; and with doves that drew thee,
Fair and fleet around the dark earth from heaven,
Dipping vibrant wings down the azure distance,
    Through the mid-ether;

Very swift they came; and thou, gracious Vision,
Leaned with face that smiled in immortal beauty,
Leaned to me and asked, "What misfortune threatened?
    Why I had called thee?"

"What my frenzied heart craved in utter yearning,
Whom its wild desire would persuade to passion?
What disdainful charms, madly worshipped, slight thee?
    Who wrongs thee, Sappho?"

"She that fain would fly, she shall quickly follow,
She that now rejects, yet with gifts shall woo thee,
She that heeds thee not, soon shall love to madness,
    Love thee, the loth one!"

Come to me now thus, Goddess, and release me
From distress and pain; and all my distracted
Heart would seek, do thou, once again fulfilling,
    Still be my ally!

LAMENT
FOR ADONIS

———————

Ah, for Adonis!
See, he is dying,
Delicate, lovely,
Slender Adonis.

Ah, for Adonis!
Weep, O ye maidens,
Beating your bosoms,
Rending your tunics.

O Cytherea,
Hasten, for never
Loved thou another
As thy Adonis.

See, on the rosy
Cheek with its dimple,
Blushing no longer,
Thanatos' shadow.

Save him, O Goddess!
Thou, the beguiler,
All-powerful, holy,
Stay the dread evil.

Ah, for Adonis!
No more at vintage
Time will he come with
Bloom of the meadows.

Ah, for Adonis!
See, he is dying,
Fading as flowers
With the lost summer.

ODE TO
ANACTORIA

———————

Peer of Gods to me is the man thy presence
Crowns with joy; who hears, as he sits beside thee,
Accents sweet of thy lips the silence breaking,
      With lovely laughter;

Tones that make the heart in my bosom flutter,
For if I, the space of a moment even,
Near to thee come, any word I would utter
      Instantly fails me;

Vain my stricken tongue would a whisper fashion,
Subtly under my skin runs fire ecstatic;
Straightway mists surge dim to my eyes and leave them
      Reft of their vision;

Echoes ring in my ears; a trembling seizes
All my body bathed in soft perspiration;
Pale as grass I grow in my passion's madness,
       Like one insensate;

But must I dare all, since to me unworthy,
Bliss thy beauty brings that a God might envy;
Never yet was fervid woman a fairer
       Image of Kypris.

Ah! undying Daughter of God, befriend me!
Calm my blood that thrills with impending transport;
Feed my lips the murmur of words to stir her
       Bosom to pity;

Overcome with kisses her faintest protest,
Melt her mood to mine with amorous touches,
Till her low assent and her sigh's abandon
       Lure me to rapture.

BRIDAL SONG

Bride, that goest to the bridal chamber
In the dove-drawn car of Aphrodite,
    By a band of dimpled
        Loves surrounded;

Bride, of maidens all the fairest image
Mitylene treasures of the Goddess,
    Rosy-ankled Graces
        Are thy playmates;

Bride, O fair and lovely, thy companions
Are the gracious hours that onward passing
    For thy gladsome footsteps
        Scatter garlands.

Bride, that blushing like the sweetest apple
On the very branch's end, so strangely
    Overlooked, ungathered
        By the gleaners;

Bride, that like the apple that was never
Overlooked but out of reach so plainly,
    Only one thy rarest
        Fruit may gather;

Bride, that into womanhood has ripened
For the harvest of the bridegroom only,
    He alone shall taste thy
        Hoarded sweetness.

CLËIS

Daughter of mine, so fair,
    With a form like a golden flower,
Wherefore thy pensive air
    And the dreams in the myrtle bower?

Clëis, beloved, thy eyes
    That are turned from my gaze, thy hand
That trembles so, I prize
    More than all the Lydian land;

More than the lovely hills
    With the Lesbian olive crowned;—
Tell me, darling, what ills
    In the gloom of thy thought are found?

Daughter of mine, come near
    And thy head on my knees recline;
Whisper and never fear,
    For the beat of thy heart is mine.

Sweet mother, I can turn
    With content to my loom no more;
My bosom throbs, I yearn
    For a youth that my eyes adore;

Lykas of Eresus,
    Whom I knew when a little child;
My heart by Love is thus
    With the sweetest of pain beguiled.

APHRODITE'S PRAISE

O Sappho, why art thou ever
Singing with praises the blessed
    Queen of the heaven?

Why does the heart in thy bosom
Ever revert in its yearning
    Throb to the Goddess?

Why are thy senses unsated
Ever in quest of elusive
    Love that is deathless?

Ah, gracious Daughter of Cyprus,
Never can I as a mortal
    Tire of thy service.

Thou art the breath of my body,
The blood in my veins, and the glowing
    Pulse of my bosom.

Omnipotent, burning, resistless,
Thou art the passion that shaking
    Masters me ever.

Thou art the crisis of rapture
Relaxing my limbs, and the melting
    Ebb of emotion;

Bringing the tears to my lashes,
Sighs to my lips, in the swooning
    Excess of passion.

O golden-crowned Aphrodite,
Grant I shall ever be grateful,
    Sure of thy favor;

Worthy the lot of thy priestess,
Supreme in the song that forever
    Rings with thy praises.

COURAGE

Faint not in thy strong heart!
    Nor downcast stand apart;
Beyond the reach of daring will there lies
    No beauty's prize.

Faint not in thy strong heart!
    Through temple, field and mart,
Courage alone the guerdon from the fray
    May bear away.

COMPARISON

Less soft a Tyrian robe
    Of texture fine,
Less delicate a rose
    Than flesh of thine.

Whiter thy breast than snow
    That virgin lies,
And deeper than the blue
    Of seas thy eyes.

More golden than the fruit
    Of orange trees,
Thy locks that floating lure
    The satyr breeze.

Less fine of silver string
    An Orphic lyre,
Less sweet than thy low laugh
    That wakes desire.

GNOMICS

I

My ways are quiet, none may find
My temper of malignant kind;
For one should check the words that start
When anger spreads within the heart.

II

Who from my hands what I can spare
Of gifts accept the largest share,
Those are the very ones who boast
No gratitude and wrong me most.

III

He who in face and form is fair
Must needs be good, the Gods declare;
But he whose thought and act are right
Will soon be equal fair to sight.

IV

Beauty of youth is but the flower
Of spring, whose pleasure lasts an hour;
While worth that knows no mortal doom
Is like the amaranthine bloom.

THE
FIRST KISS

———————

And down I set the cushion
Upon the couch that she,
Relaxed supine upon it,
Might give her lips to me.

As some enamored priestess
At Aphrodite's shrine,
Entranced I bent above her
With sense of the divine.

She had, by nature nubile,
In years a child, no hint
Of any secret knowledge
Of passion's least intent.

Her mouth for immolation
Was ripe, and mine the art;
And one long kiss of passion
Deflowered her virgin heart.

LETO
AND NIOBE

Leto and Niobe were friends full dear,
The Goddess' heart and woman's heart were one
In that maternal love that men revere,
Love that endures when other loves are done.

But Niobe with all a mother's pride,
Artless and foolish, would not be denied;
And boasted that her children were more fair
Than Leto's lovely children of the air.

The proud Olympians vowed revenge for this,
Irate Apollo, angered Artemis;
They slew her children, heedless of her moan,
And with the last her heart was turned to stone.

DAWN

Just now the golden-sandalled Dawn
Peered through the lattice of my room;
    Why must thou fare so soon, my Phaon?

Last night I met thee at the shore,
A thousand hues were in the sky;
    The breeze from Cyprus blew, my Phaon!

I drew, to lave thy heated brow,
My kerchief dripping from the sea;
    Why hadst thou sailed so far, my Phaon?

Far up the narrow mountain paths
We heard the shepherds fluting home;
    Like some white God thou seemed, my Phaon!

And through the olive trees we saw
The twinkle of my vesper lamp;
    Wilt kiss me now as then, my Phaon?

Nay, loosen not with gentle force
The clasp of my restraining arms;
    I will not let thee go, my Phaon!

See, deftly in my trailing robe
I spring and draw the lattice close;
    Is it not night again, my Phaon?

THE GARDEN
OF THE NYMPHS

———————

All around through the apple boughs in blossom
Murmur cool the breezes of early summer,
And from leaves that quiver above me gently
    Slumber is shaken;

Glades of poppies swoon in the drowsy languor,
Dreaming roses bend, and the oleanders
Bask and nod to drone of bees in the silent
    Fervor of noontide;

Myrtle coverts hedging the open vista,
Dear to nightly frolic of Nymph and Satyr,
Yield a mossy bed for the brown and weary
    Limbs of the shepherd.

Echo ever wafts through the drooping frondage,
Ceaseless silver murmur of water falling
In the grotto cool of the Nymphs, the sacred
      Haunt of Immortals;

Down the sides of rocks that are gray and lichened
Trickle tiny rills, whose expectant tinkle
Drips with gurgle hushed in the clear glimmering
      Depths of the basin.

Fair on royal couches of leaves recumbent,
Interspersed with languor of waxen lilies,
Lotus flowers empurple the pool whose edge is
      Cushioned with mosses;

Here recline the Nymphs at the hour of twilight,
Back in shadows dim of the cave, their golden
Sea-green eyes half lidded, up to their supple
      Waists in the water.

Sheltered once by ferns I espied them binding
Tresses long, the tint of lilac and orange;
Just beyond the shimmer of light their bodies
      Roseate glistened;

Deftly, then, they girdled their loins with garlands,
Linked with leaves luxuriant limb and shoulder;
On their breasts they bruised the red blood of roses
      Fresh from the garden.

She of orange hair was the Nymph Euxanthis,
And the lilac-tressed were Iphis and Io;
How they laughed, relating at length their ease in
      Evading the Satyr.

PERSEPHONE

———————

I saw a tender maiden plucking flowers
Once, long ago, in the bright morning hours;
And then from heaven I saw a sudden cloud
Fall swift and dark, and heard her cry aloud.

Again I looked, but from my open door
My anxious eyes espied the maid no more;
The cloud had vanished, bearing her away
To underlands beyond the smiling day.

THE CLIFF OF LEUCAS

———

Afar-seen cliff
Stands in the western sea
Toward Cephallenian lands.

Apollo's temple crowns
Its whitened crest,
And at its base
The waves eternal beat.

Its leap has power
To cure the pangs
Of unrequited love.

Thither pale lovers go
With anguished hearts
To dare the deep and quench
Love's slow consuming flame.

Urged to the edge
By maddening desire,
I, too, shall fling myself
Imploring thee,
Apollo, lord and king!

Into the chill
Embraces of the sea,
Less cold than thine, O Phaon,
I shall fall—
Fall with the flutter of a wounded dove;

And I shall rise
Indifferent forever to love's dream,
Or find below
The sea's eternal voice,
Eternal peace.

FRAGMENTS

Translated by Henry De Vere Stacpoole

The following poems
where first published in
Sappho: A New Rendering, 1918

MOONLIGHT

———————

The stars around the fair moon fade
Against the night,
When gazing full she fills the glade
And spreads the seas with silvery light.

LOVE

———

Sweet mother, at the idle loom I lean,
Weary with longing for the boy that still
Remains a dream of loveliness—to fill
My soul, my life, at Aphrodite's will.

SLEEP

With eyes of darkness,
The sleep of night.

THY FORM IS LOVELY

———————

Thy form is lovely and thine eyes are honeyed,
        O'er thy face the pale
Clear light of love lies like a veil.
Bidding thee rise,
With outstretched hands,
Before thee Aphrodite stands.

CLAÏS

I have a daughter,
Claïs fair,
Poised like a golden flower in air,
Lydian treasures her limbs outshine
(Claïs, beloved one,
Claïs mine!)

DICA

With flowers fair adorn thy lustrous hair,
Dica, amidst thy locks sweet blossoms twine,
With thy soft hands, for so a maiden stands
Accepted of the gods, whose eyes divine
Are turned away from her—though fair as May
She waits, but round whose locks no flowers shine.

EVENING

Children astray to their mothers, and goats to the herd,
Sheep to the shepherd, through twilight the wings of the bird,
All things that morning has scattered with fingers of gold,
All things thou bringest, O Evening! at last to the fold.

GRACE

What country maiden charms thy heart,
However fair, however sweet,
Who has not learned by gracious Art
To draw her dress around her feet?

TO HER LYRE

Singing, O shell, divine!
Let now thy voice be mine.

I LOVED THEE

———

I loved thee, Atthis, once,
    once long ago.

FRAGMENT

———————

From heaven returning;
Red of hue, his chlamys burning
Against the blue.

THE
LESBIAN SINGER

———————

Upstanding, as the Lesbian singer stands
Above the singers of all other lands.

FRAGMENT

———

Upon thy girl friend's white and tender breast,
Sleep thou, and on her bosom find thy rest.

AS WIND UPON
THE MOUNTAIN OAKS

———————

As wind upon the mountain oaks in storm,
So Eros shakes my soul, my life, my form.

GOODNESS

He who is fair is good to look upon;
He who is good is fair, though youth be gone.

THE ALTAR

And thus at times, in Crete, the women there
Circle in dance around the altar fair;
In measured movement, treading as they pass
With tender feet the soft bloom of the grass.

FRIEND

_____

Friend, face me so and raise
Unto my face thy face,
Unto mine eyes thy gaze,
Unto my soul its grace.

FOR THEE

———————

For thee, unto the altar will I lead
A white goat—
      To the altar by the sea;
And there, where waves advance and waves recede,
A full libation will I pour for thee.

THE SKY

I think not with these two
White arms to touch the blue.

NEVER ON
ANY MAIDEN

———————

Never on any maiden, the golden sun shall shine,
Never on any maiden whose wisdom matches thine.

XXXVI

—————

* * * * *

I spoke with Aphrodite in a dream.

ANGER

When anger stirs thy breast,
Speak not at all
(For words, once spoken, rest
Beyond recall).

THE CAPTIVE

———

Now Love has bound me, trembling, hands and feet,
O Love so fatal, Love so bitter-sweet.

LIKE THE
SWEET APPLE

———————

Like the sweet apple that reddens
At end of the bough—
Far end of the bough—
Left by the gatherer's swaying,
Forgotten, so thou.
Nay, not forgotten, ungotten,
Ungathered (till now).

THE
BRIDEGROOM

———————

Joy born of marriage thou provest,
Bridegroom thrice blest,
Holding the maiden thou lovest
Clasped to thy breast.

REGRET

Those unto whom I have given,
These have my heart most riven.

TO A SWALLOW

Pandion's daughter—O fair swallow,
Why dost thou weary me—
   (Where should I follow?)

THE
MOON HAS SET

———————

The moon has set beyond the seas,
And vanished are the Pleiades;
Half the long weary night has gone,
Time passes—yet I lie alone.